Grandma's visit

By Diana Vilches

To my mom,

Thank you for loving my kids the way you do

My grandma is in town visiting

She is very sweet and loves
me, my brother and sister so
much

Every day
she likes taking

me for walks

My favorite is
when we walk at

the park

where there are
lots of geese

and ducks

Squirrels and chipmunks

and birds of all kinds of colors and sizes

We love walking on the trail and saying hi to

everyone

Many people ride their bikes

Others like running

Others simply walk

enjoying the sunshine

But my favorites are
the ones who walk their

dogs

I love all kinds of dogs

Big Dogs

Small Dogs

Hairy Dogs

Skinny Dogs

My grandma
always brings

snacks for me

Then we go back home so I can take a nap

Before I wake up my brother and
sister come home from school

After I wake up, we all eat lunch together

My grandma always makes the
most delicious food

Then, she helps my brother ans sister with their homework

and mommy
and daddy
come home
from work

While mommy
and daddy
spend time
with grandma

I play with
my brother and
sister

Then we all eat dinner together

When grandma visits she likes

putting us to bed

Me first, because I am the youngest

Then my sister...

She loves reading books before bed

And my older brother is last

He loves hearing stories from when she was little

We love it when grandma visits

Our grandma is the best!

Made in the USA
Monee, IL
13 August 2022

11579574R00019